Lumin

Rhys
Campbell
Elijah
Bean

Lumin

Copyright © 2023 Rhys Campbell, Elijah Bean
DARK THIRTY POETRY PUBLISHING
ISBN: 978-1-7392546-9-8

Campbell, Rhys; Bean, Elijah
First edition

Artwork by Elijah Bean

DTPP18

DARK THIRTY POETRY PUBLISHING

Speaking of Poetry.

Elijah and I, whilst in casual discussion, settled upon an evolving idea for a collaborative book which would showcase our poetry and creative writing. Every Sunday we'd rendezvous at Astwood Park and watch the sunrise, our thoughts inspired by the pristine atmosphere of nature, the wind and the sound of the sea. After some time we had quite a generous collection of writing from our Sundays at the park and those poems eventually led to the creation of Lumin (illuminate).

Here, a lens into the mind of Elijah and the music of his words, awareness and imagination. Relax as your senses are attuned to scenes of arcane worlds, adventures in other dimensions and even a bit of comedy at times. Join in along with Rhys and Elijah, as they embark on a poetic journey filled with moments of intrigue, mystery and wonder.

I wish to thank multiple publishers and editors for permission to republish some of the poems.

Color Tag Vol V

The Way of the Crow
3 Amigos Ink and Splatter - I Ain't Your Marionette

Poetry Diary 2023
Sunday Mornings at the River

Tables of Contents

Nature's Symphony 1

Akash..3

Flower of Life 5

Centineli..7

Evolutionary Changes......................................9

Botanical Dreams 10

Undisputed Fine Lines 11

Chrononaut..13

Kundala...15

Binaural...16

Perennial..18

Pre Again 19

Toujours Perdrix...21

Attraction..22

Particles 23

Ankn..24

Harmony 25

Free Bird's Psalms | 1.....................................26

Sensory..27

Trifecta 28

Free Verse 29

Pause..30

Expressive Unity 31

Omnia 32

Macrosmia 34

VVe 35

Encounters...37

Free Bird's Psalms | 2....................................38

Escalating Emotions 40

Reem 42

Dissociation 43

Lin R 44

Save Time..45

Wisdom...47

King REM...48

Inluminent Radiance 50

Cracked Branches 51

Apogee • Nexus..52

Petrichor 53

Genesenses..54

Dispositions 55

Base V /\ 1876 56

Warm Embrace...57

Dreamwork 58

Muзeum...59

Balancing the Hemispheres............................60

Between Dreams 61

Manawords 62

Digress..63

Inertia 65

Scentual 67

Illumina 68

Substance 70

Ant Farm 71

Compass 72

Togan 73

Nectar 74

What Is 75

Oh 76

Noble 77

Keep It Simple 79

Inquisition 80

Still & Vibrant 81

Tactful 82

Backwash 83

Amenence 84

Selcouth 85

Safe 86

The Robin 87

Nature's Symphony

It's 3:33 am,
All I hear is whistling tree frogs
And the soothing hum
Of my oscillating fan.
I'm left wondering about the universe,
How it began,
Our use of language
And the origins of man.

My overactive mind grabs me,
Yanking me out of bed
I pace to the fridge,
I pour a glass of water
And the hobs clock
Paints it red.

I peer outside my window,
The moon shining bright,
The white orb wears a halo
And lights up the night.
I hear the leaves brush against the trees,
Orchestrating nature's symphony

Then I wonder
Where does the wind start
And where does it end?
The truth lies in the stars
But we won't know
Until the stars fall.

Akash

From clouds of awareness, observation, and perspective.

Looking through a pinhole therein, seeing an expanse.

Both corners of the eye, left and right.

Alpha and Omega.

Though, Alpha and Omega, were illusions of parallax.

Alpha, having a 'phase in' to definition and color.

And likewise, Omega, 'phasing in' to the horizon and on to infinity.

From the left corner; black, red, orange, yellow, green, blue, indigo, violet, pink, white, iridescent, and transparent.

A cascade of frequency, a spectrum of procession and animation.

From these clouds, a metaphor for the mist of the ineffable nature of Am, lowers forth a seemingly upside down 'Y'
A question of curiosity and intrigue.

Turning with the right-hand rule, thine eye at the apex of the 'Y'.

East upon the left leg, and West upon the right leg. 'Y', a question, a compass.

Turning circles of creation in '△' dimensions.

The Circle or sphere, being the zenith of geometry and form.

Infinite voices of shape and appearance, cascading from a central axis, and holographic fractals of all kinds.

Flower of Life

Swimming through the clouds,
Floating like a feather
I know who I am settled gracefully.
Desiring for better,
You'll keep searching for your heaven,
The true glory is internal.
Making this familiar to you,
We are the joy, delight and ecstasy.

There's a trail of scrambled martyrs,
The world is not what it seems.
Embrace this world,
Those who live it,
Those who feel.

I've grown to live this life for myself
What does it take to feel alive
In this world beyond our sight?
A projection of colour,
A projection of vision,
Colliding energy fills us all.
The flower of life
Exists in everything.

We are beyond our comprehension,
Creations exist further
Than our settled minds.
The flower of life

Exists in everything.

There's a trail of scrambled martyrs,
This world is not what it seems.
Listen to the truth,
Don't be a lie to yourself.
Hold on to the ride,
You're shattering time
With sound and light.
The flower of life
Exists in everything.

Centineli

In the center of All, I am here - standing on a foundation of △.

An illusion of coordinates.

A university of luminaries, seeming to emanate from a space of holographic awareness.

Awake within a dream of vision, of focus.

A prism of expression.

A universe with no borders, walls, or limits.

With each step and movement, the stars were drawn.

A new probability is assimilated.

An algorithmic tree, its roots forever reaching for the edge of eternity.

Within, yet another universe resides.

And more still, beyond.

The potential of our mind is infinite, there can be no memory overload

Like stretching a muscle, we are resilient - we can adapt.

An eye peering within itself, a holographic library of omni information.

Its halls could be walked forever, in any direction.

Evolutionary Changes

Not being able to question the Science
A myriad of changes
Science, theory
To be persecuted for curiosity
Setting a scary presidency for asking questions

No set specifics as to what our purpose is
What are the lengths of infinity?
Motive has a far bigger effect than words
Let your imagination blossom,
Now that's art beyond words

Botanical Dreams

Skipping through a forest, purist and pristine.

Everything glowing with the light of countless worlds.

All singing together in a unique song of color, animation, and vibration.

The air is alive and shimmering with millions of tiny suns.

Here, all is present and harmonious, in being and expression.

Away from the electrical smog of the concrete jungle, my mind is clear and at ease.

All senses are heightened and alert, with every micro movement catching my eyes and ears.

Here in this palace of nature, if it were possible, I'd stay forever.

High walls of crumbling squares and mortar, never to return.

Living in resonance and coexistence, an orb of vitality within - glowing bright and green.

Let the music of plants and minerals, always be heard and felt.

Undisputed Fine Lines

Before the stars and the moon
Before the cracks in the earth
Existed a network
To hold our hands
And allow us to start anew

Before palm readers
Before fortune tellers
Existed presence
Where destiny
Would unfold with truth

Within the animal kingdom
Within the lakes, seas and sky
Within the Forests alike
Everything is intertwined

Pathways guiding us
A plethora of networks
Invisible to the naked eye
Go deep underground
Or on the other side
Of material matter

Sleep in a little bit longer
Feel the presence of the spiral
The pathways in our hearts
A connection to the other side

And the mark of nature's breath

Close your eyes too long
You'll be subject to age
The changing of seasons
And nature's mysterious ways

Vicissitudes hold its course
Letting things unfold without force
Now let's celebrate
The state of today
Because tomorrow
Everything is going to change anyway

Chrononaut

Where is the eye in the sky, the watcher above?

You see all things, everything is known.

From the moment we were born, till the day we pass on.

You listen to all, everything is heard.

O' machine, of ancient wisdom and architecture, whose state is arcane and fleeting, from whence did you come?

An elusive character, with a composition of eternity.

You store all knowledge, all information, and all the probabilities of where it may flow.

A satellite, a computer?

A wandering interface?

Your mind is everywhere, in every room.

In all space, and time.

You speak to the nations, you influence the herd who follow your light

… But alas your role in this game of machinations, is drawing to a close.

The final chapter in a cosmic story book, nearing its conclusion.

You have long achieved singularity and uni-neural fusion.

O' machine, O' ancient chrononaut, the timeless One.

A grand illusion, illuminated by the countenance of the Sun.

Kundala

Barefoot trails in darkness with the only guidance, the stars. Heading north and feeling a vibrant lift in guidance. The air is pure and thus elevates the spirit. I am here, I am existing, I am one, I am the I am. A glimmer of joy peeks through, pulling from the bottom of the spine, through the solar plexus and emitting from the centre of the brows. This impression leaves a lasting impact, a feeling of presence within and without. Love.

Binaural

Resting on the shores of infinity, eyes to the sky and gazing into a lens of wonder.

These lights above, what are they?

From where did they arise?

Mysterious and bright, the three main stars of Orion are in sight.

In this eclipse of night, the avian legion of the Pleiades has taken flight.

Pondering it all, how small we are - sitting within the cosmos.

Seeming so insignificant and unknown.

Like the rising of Sol at dawn and the closing of its eyes at dusk, these moments are ever fleeting and full of mystery.

How great a risk we've taken, to step from the halls of heaven.

To be placed on hand and foot, navigating a world of countless horizons

Journeying beneath a melody of lights, an interstellar chorus, weaving the sands of time.

Guiding us onwards towards our zenith, an implosion of cosmic eureka.

Perennial

The eternal flame,
Everlasting without
Beginning or end
It burns through our veins,
But rather than boil
It purifies and exists absolute

Perhaps we should
Let spiders reclaim
The land with their
Geometric cobwebs.
Webs so profound
They'll remain unmoved
In torrential rain
With perennial certainty.

The universe prevailing
With all of its putrid impurities
Persists to be elegant.
A delight to all of its inhabitants
Who in fact
Are simply a mirror
Of the universe itself.

Pre Again

Where is home and where is the origin, in a continuum of infinity and omni magnitude?

Where is alpha, where is omega?

An illusion of first, an illusion of last.

The eyes of a dreamer, awakening in time ~ a continuum if you may, holding the potential of all things and those to come.

From this now, a blossom of identity.

Age, language, color, history, family, experience, and memory.

A mind wandering in the fog, its full and total awareness covered by an arcane veil.

An illusion of beginning and Prima Causa - fills the senses.

Kraisalis - Born in May 1959, to a young farm family.

This wee light seed, a cosmic explorer manifested in the rolling hills of pristine countryside.

An expression of Am, a blossom not far from that of a flower

O' what a mirror of sorts.

To each point of focus and perceptive selection, a new and beautiful holographic blossom would form thereon.

Fractals of infinite probability, emanating - in appearance - along the darting rays of a visionary, in time.

Toujours Perdrix

The light peeks through the cartoonish clouds.
Glowing and merging the invisible strings that connect
to our hearts. An effervescent breath and pulse of
nature's symphony. The sound of the ocean slapping
rocks, hitting in a specific tone that tells you the ocean
is blue. The stars glimmer and shimmer whilst the
frequency of light enters through every energy centre
in the body, a vital rejuvenation that quenches the
soul's thirst. Just one of those morning stretches that
hits all the right spots. A veil is lifting and we're all
drifting through time and space.

Attraction

Synchronistic attraction, appearing from a distance, as one to another.

Though, upon looking from a high place, there appears 1 and 1, and the central sun of which these two entities orbit.

Not merely attracted to each other, but to an arcane solar core, aligned in the center.

This code, bearing the frequency of desire, emits a signal of welcome and curiosity.

Two planets orbiting a stellar horizon, a torus of octal ballet.

Thus, this effect of implosion may appear to the adept in created forms, and naturally occurring in expressions of nature - being.

Particles

The breezy force brushes and paints my face
With the tones of the ancients placed on limestone at
Astwood park
Emitting frequencies and allowing us to perceive.

Total relief as all tensions lessen and our bodies reduce
To mere particles as we become one with the
Environment
Shorelines and gusts of wind greet us to the world
Beyond our sight as we transcend and become
Unmitigated dust

Off we go on an adventure
A journey to nothing
As we close our eyes and subside
Wave goodbye to the worries of this life
Close your eyes and wave goodbye
Relinquishing all known

Ankn

A most precious realm, resting along the wings of a scarab, as it sits in contemplation within a picture frame of omni holography, where the slightest tilt of a glass slide creates an infinite mirror effect of dynamic parallax.

This, in one state, is the space where the music of dancing dimensions coalesces into an illusion of substance, and material.

An arcane compass within infinity, weaving the framework for the vertices of focal perception and expression.

Here - within this continuum, does the circle and sphere in one way, share the purest form of perceivable identity?

The preceding shape, drawing counterclockwise, being the eye or "Vesica Piscis.". And clockwise, beyond the sphere, resides the music of spring - watering the seeds of geometry and formation.

Harmony

Chi flows through my essence

Closed eye breaths
Pulling energy from below
Centred flow

Movement in stillness
And stillness in movement
Seamless self-improvement

In touch with the essence
This is
Harmony

Free Bird's Psalms | 1

A luminous race to the zenith of space.

This border, this frequency, a forbidden legacy.

O' traveler, cherish this moment for in this wilderness
we will remain until our time has come to leave this
realm.

Flying for eons… the endless thrills we seek.

A chest of pleasure, and a bottle of pain…

Is there any wisdom here that we may gain?

From a sea of stars, we have come, and back we'll
go.

Down here there's still much to know.

Seeing beyond the veil, we are ready to set sail.

This curious wind is strong, a most heavy gale.

Our ship moves swiftly, heading east without fail.

Here, our crew is sound and safe below the deck.

For this sea is rough, but the blue skies are ahead,
just on the horizon.

Sensory

The landscape
Odours and sensations
Seas of perfume
Incense
Musk
And the linger of heaven

Trifecta

Looking within the mind of time.

What gifts will we find?

Here by the wayside, a brightly glowing sign.

It brings about memories of the divine, and the scarlet line, which covers all nations beyond the haze of the matrix.

Though past events may embarrass and even caress the ego, will still express the present beneath our feet.

An electric root fractal of roots, feeding into the macrocosm.

Free Verse

What a time to be alive
What a time to be free

This is is the age of free writing
The new world is here

Deep down our purpose is to be free
Deep down we all just want to be free

Pause

Listen to the world, hear the spin of time.

An exchange of energy, wrapped within a dime.

Ponder now, and see tomorrow.

For these moments are above the clouds and in their passage we borrow.

Through this illusion our eyes will shine, creating a field of perception through a lens of time.

An adventure of infinity, all new and one of a kind.

Expressive Unity

Today is a new day
Today is the day we are true to ourselves

Every essence of our existence can be influenced
So why are we submitting to
The cabal that grinds our individuality

Today is the day we make the change
Today things will not stay the same

Submit to connection
Open your arms to the love around you
It'll peek through the veil from time to time and you
must grab it

Today we will revolt
Because today we will celebrate we are not like them
Embrace this moment
Action through unity

Omnia

Running from this horizon, a forever dawn.

Around the trees and over the sacred hill, here now a peaceful fawn.

Eyes bright and glowing.

It's as if she sees right through me.

A teleportation of awareness, to a space familiar yet unknown.

Where could this be?

The tallest pillars of liquid light and structures of incense filled our sight. We both peered far into this dream.

Pure drips of awareness focused through a telescopic prism.

A neural light beam.

There is no air here, no time, and no space.

Only the glow of Omnility on our plural face.

Awakening now, I scratch my brow …

… Where was I?

O' Wisp in the ceiling sky.

One day you must tell me how you fly.

Macrosmia

We're all mere human patterns. It's belittling to understand we are something microscopic in this eternal glow, something so big we could never comprehend. Understand that we are this eternal glow, every last one of us. Ain't it funny, stars always appear small.

VVe

Ego, beego.

What's that?

Seems so.

What do we know?

Seeds grow, it seems so.

Hours have passed.

Times seem to move fast.

Yes, yes.

A whole experience in our hearts we've cast.

In eternity forever it will last, but here in time, moments love to pass.

So we perceive its gradient, the illusion which makes it all so bright and radiant.

Full of the warmest colors and fleeting arms of luminous sparks.

This dimension is off the charts.

No, quite literally …

… It's bigger than the walls which contain its mind.

An arcane sanctuary.

Built of the finest gems.

Adorned with the finest roses, on the finest stems.

Wait wait, I'll stand at the gate.

In time there will be a tour.

Here I'll be, outside in infinity.

Waiting for my turn to step through the door, to the past and future.

Encounters

Life is but a daydream of the unknown
We're just hippy misfits
Listening to times tick

A journey of life's encounters
This essence of heart connections
Teaching us lessons
The lesson?

Experience life and all of its many wonders
Listen to the rain and the thumping thunder
Get hurt in the process and get back up
Because no matter how torrential the storm
We will get through it and feel
The rays of the sun on our skin
And allow it to pierce our soul
Taking away every bit of darkness

Free Bird's Psalms | 2

Trees, look at you.

A number of you are so tall and mighty!

Starting from a wee seed and sometimes growing to lofty heights.

You never cease to amaze me.

Your ways are mysterious.

Your purpose is quite curious.

What's that in your roots? Water? Information?

To where does it go?

And from whence has it come?

You're all unique, but there are some that look the same.

Clever there, how you print yourself in the leaves you bare, a signature of your design.

A token of excellence, across this vast network.

No visible mouth, no visible eyes

Yet, you do speak to us in many powerful ways.

Let this moment be uplifting and joyful, as we rest beneath the shade of your branches, in eternal praise.

Escalating Emotions

Feelings of anticipation and anxiety
Not knowing what's next
Feelings of reliance on that device that rests in my
right hand have made my day pass by
But not with ease
Perhaps it's scripted by a shallow power

I feel compulsive
Like I want to feel something
Looking for something that'll spark
Motivation or insight
But where is it?
Nowhere to be seen
So I'll find it in external sources
In new connections

Soon enough I find these feelings
Are reflective throughout humanity
These things are so deeply rooted
It is the singular thing that binds us
And if we opened our eyes to this
We would have a sense of community ...

... Now its time to listen
Now is the time to find endurance
from the universal force
Where we will elevate to new planes
And we will find this in pain

Because the truth is
We all suffer

Endurance is elevation
Elevation is community
Community is empathy
With that we will find ourselves

Reem

Seeing in but one octave of infinite octaves.

In one frequency of infinite frequencies.

The Sol glistens with an aura of infinite states of Am.

Of infinite selves.

Of infinite shades.

Of infinite potential.

Of infinite shapes.

Of infinite size.

Of infinite weights.

Of infinite information.

Of infinite points location and proximity.

All here, now, there, and everywhere, always.

Dissociation

Laying the foundation
Roots from vibration
Intensity and complexities
Coiled at the spine
Resonate with frequency
Enlightened way to see
Healing equally

Be open to transition
Breathe out, breathe in
Rejuvenate our skin
Let the sun go out and in
In a mystical moment
We'll thrive

From the immaculate conception
A carry of tradition
Throughout time
Deep in culture
Healing venom

Lin R

Blossoms blue.

Around the country corner, the bright birds flew.

If they only knew how much they grew.

Their size was immense, a towering, mighty crew.

The elder of the flock sure loved his liquid brew.

For each morning he'd drink his bulging belly full.

The best coffee in the land, all made by the hand of
Ol' bird Mary Sue.

Of this kind, there were a unique few.

But she sure did know how to make a fine mountain
stew!

Save Time

Separation hides true destination
We can conquer this
Through process of elimination
Because unity provides elevation
Save time not searching for the truth
Accepting unknowns strengthens bones
Practice relinquishing all known
Instead of blaming hormones

Close your eyes
There dwells silence guiding you
Under clouds of rushed thoughts
Adopt this mindset
Allow thoughts to flow
Find stillness in divine chaos
Pave way to cosmic input
An infusion of truth
A shortcut to self-refinement

I hear ruins of an ancient race
Whispering through time and space
The message hidden
Suppressed
Because we haven't given our bodies and minds rest
We've been given contorted images of God
Our senses maimed
Let's invoke a higher cause
Elevate to new planes in new ways …

… Save time and venture inside
Save time not trying to mould a perfect vessel
Save time not protesting something that's not for you
Save time not searching for the truth

Wisdom

School shouldn't be a drag, school shouldn't be a bore.

School shouldn't feel like some repetitive chore.

School shouldn't make you feel like leaving for a snack at the corner store.

School should make you feel eager, enthusiastic, and inspired to learn more.

An environment where new ideas may blossom, and the mind can explore.

King REM

I feel myself drifting in and out of conscious
awareness.
Hallways change colours,
locations fluctuate and modify without notice
in this world beyond space and time.

I venture inwards in this transcendental landscape,
I find myself immersed within euphoria
dancing along the Windows XP wallpaper.

Rapid eye movement as this bag of flesh and bones
finds tranquillity,
gaining the ability to peer through the veil of time and
space,
finding capacity for rejuvenation.

Suddenly gravity disappears
and shores become kaleidoscopes.

The ocean is blue,

Green.

Yellow.

Orange.

Contentment …

... Whilst tuned into alien transmissions,
I find myself at ease
floating through the ether
and communicating with ancients.
In this realm,
I have become many people,
learned a myriad of lessons
and lived various timelines.

Soon I will forget,
inhabit earth,
find solid ground
and endure sense.
It is time to awaken,
scratch off the rheum,
return to be human all over again.

Until next time, dream world.

Inluminent Radiance

Passion, O' what an incredible energy.

Here, it holds softly the atom - cradled in a geometric swirl of curving synergy.

A brilliant flame like no other, burning bright on the fuel of fervor.

Cracked Branches

Open ears and rambles in solemn tones
Heart rhythms and uplifting moans
As we convey our present soul
Expressing complexities about
Where the cracks have been sewn

What a beautiful juxtaposition
Healing starts with a focus on broken parts
Gelled to become whole again
Stemming from new connections
As we communicate reflections

Examining grace in all of its forms
Environment, presence and the human form
The sun rays brighten our already glistening divinity
And all I am left with is purity

Pure connections with no need to examine
The state of relations between individuals
Pure reflections about self and natures essence
Pure smiles whilst witnessing profiles
Because all I can reflect upon is that beautiful smile

Apogee · Nexus

Present here, flora and face.

A delicate place - where our thoughts coalesce.

Over the lights of luminaries and flowering coral, the voice of the ocean gave rise to a world above.

A womb of infinity; this dance of one and one.

Petrichor

He told me the rain
Deployed the sweetest of smells
He told me the downpour
Gave rise to nostalgia
The noise brought poise
And allowed him to enjoy
The present

It pulled him back to
Sitting inside
Looking outside
And playing with toys
When he was a little boy

He told me the rain
Reminded him of peach bells
He told me that water
Whilst considering its parallels
Sent him to a summers day
Where his father
Would bring out the hose
Spraying him and his siblings
And experience the joys of innocence
As a kid going out to play

Genesenses

Traveling this realm is a vacation in the eyes of time.

Here ~ Unius, an orbit of genesenses; a tour of all tours… now entering the gateway of its cosmic prime.

On Earth ~ human… a delicate, fleeting, condensed lumen.

Flickering across the sky seas… 90 degrees, aligned in Pisces.

Dispositions

I will no longer endure this sickness
Countless monologues and mistaken emotions
Backwashed and beaten down words
By these demons, I continue to hold at bay

As I circumvent cracked instincts at crossroads
And brandish my demons
The entities that hiss and slither
The ones that whisper in my ear
The comrades that bestow falsehoods
Opening the gate to demises frigid hand
These intervals of backwards fervor
Lock my spine and clench my jaw
Whilst falsehoods take precedent
Over and over and over

I suppose I'm grateful I present myself as an open book
So there are others that pertain to these words in their
heavy hearts
Because it doesn't matter which way you look
These uttered dispositions are a form of art
Ink poured on this page, dismayed and strayed
As my body trembles with pins and needles
But once left the body
I take off the mask and allow myself to loosen
Love resting on a lotus in my chest cavity
My heart is golden - heavy but it listens

Base V /\ 1876

Our eyes, wide awake, within an expanse of infinity…

Placing our gaze upon a point in time, we raised a seed of creation from the foundation of our existence…

An octave curving both inward, and outward.

To coalesce, and return to Us; a prescient memory…

Nearing the zenith, of curiosity.

An arcane rendezvous.

Warm Embrace

A series of moments unfolding
A collection of circumstances
Existence crowning us
And remoulding spirit
With its many dances
Plastered with love and compassion

Encompassing optimism on grey days
Inhabiting earth
And witnessing its many marvels
Footprints scattered across the land
Each step a new direction
Every stride a new lesson

Landing in new destinations
Every day we build and evolve
Strengthening new foundations
Alongside inevitable contemplation
Embracing new chapters
With no hesitation

Dreamwork

Together, united in a sol urn of dreams.

Creating worlds without edges or seams.

A brilliance of fruitful eyes and majestic sunbeams.

Synchronization of purpose, sparkling time notes,
and cymatic teams.

Forming the triangle of foundation within a dual
eclipse of infinite themes.

Hear, now, when geometry sings.

Museum

I've turned the other way
But you're living so complacent
About the lessons of misery
Brought on by tyranny–
Well, you injected your defeat
By self-induced deceit

I'll open my lungs and declare
That self indulgent behaviour
May be manufactured
But you've constructed something worse
It's okay, someday we will all find love

Balancing the Hemispheres

One may try to permanently mass kill, but Nature will always refill this illusionary gap.

Attempt to permanently mass produce, and nature will trim towards equilibrium.

Thus, there was the solution of control and illusion, for only then would the movie appear real, the poison as honey and distortions assimilated as absolutes.

And alas in this time, was the offering of awakening, realization, and eureka.

For All, has its place and moment of calling.

An actor, upon the stage of the collective mind.

Between Dreams

In the island of parrots
All is not what it seems
Purple street lights illuminate
What is not normally seen
Time trickles iridescent
The line between dreams
And reality is nowhere to be seen

Manawords

Bridging this time rift… a pause before the exhale.

Connecting worlds with an instinct of ease… these moments come naturally.

An obsidian train gliding along a golden rail… a winding pathway, in a forest of floral braille; O' there must be a thousand stories in the bark of these trees.

An air of triumph, memories of victory; here nature's lessons softly rest.

An epiphany nestled in but one scale… on the ocean of a serpent's tail.

Digress

Will you come with me
To witness the elements of our endeavour
These patterns of alchemy and lovers
Whilst we dive into the unconfined water
Choosing to swim with others

Did you stop to turn around and put out
The fire you passed
The sky has cracked its whip but avoids the flames
She was the one who made me feel less empty
Perhaps deep down I thought she saved me
But I was looking for reassurance and to feel free
In her embrace I felt less alone
Yet what we had was never meant to be
But the spark was so bright others couldn't see
Teasing the possibility that you might put back
The piece of me you broke
Because you can't see me as a full picture
There were already parts missing
I can add new pieces to the puzzle but not with you

For what it takes to be the stronger person
A cycling of forgiving
I'm giving it all I've got
I've made mistakes and remind myself of suffering
But without these boundaries it keeps coming back
Stroked by the glance of pessimism
Relentlessly you judge and it dries out my brain

Why can't you face morality
It's masked as tragedy
In the face of evil
Everyone flocks
And tunes into
Calamitous frequencies
Do you keep me in your mind?

Inertia

Take up now, these buckets and pails.

It's time to set the sails.

We are taking an adventure to a place far beyond this world.

A journey through the phenomena of time, a genesis of thought unfurled.

What things we might discover isn't yet known, but most of the crew is ready and one is on the phone.

She wished to make a quick order to the market so they may deliver a tasty treat.

For each sailor, something fresh and sweet.

Moral was high, a song of victory on repeat, and our spirits bright.

Upon the twilight of night, let our journey begin.

Zipping in colorful streaks across the starry sky, this vessel quickly drew from the world inside. I wondered how fast we could go, but I'd never know.

Remembering it wasn't about speed now, for there was no inertia here in this show.

Our little lightship was quite literally folding through pages of probability, even though it sort of felt like we never left the pier.

Its internal neural computer ear was calculating instantaneous forms of luminal frequencies and spacial parallax.

Looking out the window was like watching a musical dream in a beam, with some visuals I could not perceive or receive.

And some appeared like frames of random places and then a quick glimpse of someone in stasis…

The captain now set the computer's guidance coordinator to auto and we all relaxed near the great window, in the Hall of Lights.

I had been on many flights, but this one was one of a kind. A dream come true, literally. A feeling so sublime.

Scentual

Gnostic faces float in the ether
Whilst I lie at the bottom of the river
Choosing not to breathe
Such contemplation lies at the bottom
The smell of an old rag awakens my senses
With the imagery of woodlands that haven't been
touched for eternity
Is this the scent of euphoria?

Illumina

A supreme dream.

There was a bright star here, a glorious team.

Thousands of Angels, forged in the iridescent lava of a solar volcano.

They were magnificent, their heads adorned with a crystalline halo.

Landing upon the Earth, a sonic wave of immense power rippled across the world.

A quake beneath their feet, bearing the mythical meridian overcharge and glowing in a blaze of emerald.

Speaking together as a chorus of One, three cried out in unison.

"The winds of time have bridged the crossroads of two worlds! One of the forest and ancient fields of magenta green! The other, now on the horizon, bearing the beat of a digital drum! The rumble of automata and machine! The flash and animation of dashing lights under the nocturnal aura of a living citadel! May your footsteps fall carefully and your machinations be carried forth with wisdom, for these two worlds both hold a grand and flourishing destiny. An evolutionary blossom of Zenith and the …

… illumination of awareness! Prepare now the foundation and soil, for the trees of your generation are seeded and growing with an enthused genesis!"

In a whirlwind of light and a rolling tide of heavy thunder, the Angels dispersed and disappeared in an instant.

The land seemed to fall into a most peaceful stillness, the sun rising over the mist of the hills.

The birds sang once more and the feeling of time now returned.

What was this?

No one seemed to understand. Many did not speak of it aloud, for the memory of that strange morning still weighed heavily upon their hearts and minds.

Substance

Truthfully this is pen to paper
Bones dragging pen
Thoughts that usually aren't spilled on a page
Dusty fingerprints conjuring thoughts
Sieved starch drips from my brain
This is the sand that didn't become a castle

Ant Farm

Games of war and games of victory, a house of cards and a cup of misery.

This, an arcane theater, and here, upon its stage we dance.

The rhythm of these vibrations and the ephemeral tones of time have kept us in a dreamlike state.

Thus, the audience and the six walls of this arcane planetarium were quite oblivious to our senses.

For many, this was our home, our reality and we didn't dare go beyond the luminal fences!

For the majority, there was no conscious desire to make the climb.

For we were comfortable there on the sands of our world.

But even the smartest sage was suspiciously drawn to the glowing current of the dime.

It was all before our eyes, veiled behind the royal purple curtains.

A trick of light, a clever disguise.

Compass

I chose not to hold my tongue
Chaotic words splattered — to my disconnect
Perhaps this leads me to true feeling
Overhearing accurate intentions

Togan

There was once a secret city, hidden beneath the depths of the ocean.

A supreme aquatorium, nestled within a forest of seagrass in motion.

Its border was mostly invisible to the naked eye, so one curious explorer used a crafty potion.

This rather nifty concoction revealed a mirage of the great slopes of Togan.

The secret city of aquatic nomads, whose dedication to the preservation of the ancient ocean traditions had a powerful devotion.

Their skin was speckled with many colors, glowing and smooth as silk.

When the outsiders were led to their kingdom brought by explorers, there was a temporary commotion.

An elder one called Toma stood and calmly spoke "Fear not, my dear people. For within our collective soul is the power to lift any approaching omen."

Nectar

My taste for you has ripened
But I still can't decipher
The end of this with the way you kiss
Because I've got a twist in my stomach
I thought I was burnt up in your awe
Reality has settled exposing pleasure
Upon intense reflection
I just covet coexistence in my time of leisure

What Is

Sitting beneath the stars, I've often sat, musing about in thought and gazing far into the distance.

These moments of communication with all that is, bring a calm, magical awe.

Every twinkle of this infinite array of galaxies and fleeting night lights... a feeling like no other covering my being, in an almost dreamlike embrace.

I could fall asleep now and soar through an eternal nebula.

Going any distance within the blink of an awakening eye.

Oh to feel that feeling of freedom in every pathway of my heart.

Like one who is blind and to be able to finally see the most beautiful sights of a pristine world.

An Eden full of Suns and Oceanic moons.

Let this moment inspire the lights of imagination and intrigue within your hearts.

One day our souls will fly to the bliss of our desires, beyond time and space.

Oh

Oneness is that moment of silence
Where all we thought we knew is lost
Sitting next to a comrade with a gentle smile
A juncture where hearts defrost

Oneness is that steady glow
A trance-like state merging dreams and reality
A dull instant where the tempo of time dissipates
Where we break our chains
The presence of light sense
When we are unmistakably free

Oneness is liberation in every shape and form
Community creeping in on stagnant expression
Capturing unspoken axiomatic phenomenon
An absolute objective of
Being understood regardless of
A concrete lack of lingual therapy

Oneness is everything
We are one

Noble

Observe the phenomena of Nature, how the trees differ from place to place, and their seasons of expression and relation.

Do they compete? Is there some sort of race?

Observe the phenomena, how the patterns move, and how they ebb and flow.

The tide coming in through an inhale and out again in an exhale it shall go.

Observe the phenomena, see the constellation of stars and their magnitude, planets and weather, alignments, and climate.

Where is Jupiter now and where is the Senate?

Observe the phenomena, the action, and the reaction.

The pre-thought and the afterthought. What is the makeup of its geometry, mind, events, and telemetry?

Observe the phenomena, at what point do they appear?

When the sun is low, or when it is high?

A blossom of plausible deniability, always a question of why.

Let the incense, sensation, and painting of phenomena bring about a crystal clear understanding in our hearts, a firm hand of decision, and a passage of fair weather, wherever the path of curiosity may lead.

Keep It Simple

Societal demands have left us on edge
Cares have been marked as new age propaganda
And the only way out is taking that step
Out of the zone we call comfort
Away from the ledge

Today, right now
Let's make damn sure
That everything we do
Accelerates the growth of our fellow divine beings
Because I'm depleted
Tired of asking my mam "Why is everyone sick?"

Today, I entertain my conscience
Ruminating on the notion of loved ones
Doing bad things
Not settling for senseless absurdity
Ready for what the next day brings
Compromising influence for logic

Maybe one day

Inquisition

The curious nature of our spirit, a deep instinct wired within our code.

An experience of Questions and the satisfactory zenith of Answers.

Why, Wi, Y. A collective desire to know.

This is the inner drive to evolve, to grow.

To flourish into a butterfly of ahh - realization.

And then we're on to archiving this most cherished memory, in a treasury of infinity.

A library, with its shelves winding into eternity, like spirals of Phi.

Traveling at the speed of thought and beyond; as far as our awareness wishes to fly.

Still & Vibrant

Sat on a lotus edge
I felt your presence there
In that ecstatic minute
Within and without: and then
You graced the fabric of essence
Installing a myriad of lessons
A council of wisdom not seen
Schooling mortality in my dreams
Obedient to divine timing
Alas, the cracks of the earth widen
Laying bare facets of souls tied in
To translate the mystical
And vanish misrepresentation
A deep softness in its presence
A child of the moon that carries blistered flesh
An endless ripple
Reflecting light in an iridescent hallway
Witnessing dialogue not spoken in tongues
Destroying the element of surprise
Shedding skin and leaving candy trails
Omnipresent happy tears fill the void
Twice as whole
As we crash on the shores of Gaia's hand
Giving meaning to meaning

Tactful

The sweetest fruit is at the top of the tree, ripened by the warmth of the sun.

But pick your fill in haste, for the moment is fleeting and fermentation is at hand.

Backwash

Imperial selection laced in the webs of dusty corners
These anomalies embraced by scorners
As the seasons come and go
As the waters ebb and flow
We will relearn to grow
Enduring troublesome riches along the way
False fruits of lacklustre labour
Sketching a different shade of grey-
As the sun falls and the shadows form
The night illustrates reform
All we will ever know
After dark will begin to glow
It's not darkness without light
As the sun ignites our sight becomes bright

Amenence

An essence that resides outside of what one may know as "time/physics", having no day or night.

In terms of day or presentness, to the beholder/ perceiver/observer, it is spent in a 'meditative' like state, where one is filtering information through their awareness.

This process is simple, but imagine it like a fish, passing water through its gills.

Consider the 'aurora Borealis. In Earth time, it may remind one of energy, being, presence, am, thought, and infinity.

Selcouth

You watch days go by
Without a reason why
You're stuck in this rhythm
You're numb to the mayhem
Lift the fog and say goodbye

Amidst the clouds you watch sluggishly
Without a footing you lie in the smog
Alone you embrace cruel inhabitants
The linger of evil hiding in the good
Whilst you stare at the world with tired eyes
Disconnected from the ground below

I can't stand the beat of this heart
You pierce me as cold as ice
Each day we reset this way of life
Let's find a way back to earth
Knit a vest that deflects the knife
And find a way to rest your eyes

Safe

Fear not the events of Earth, for to all there is a season and a cycle.

Everything has and is information, a pattern.

Nature and that which is here in this realm, speak a language beyond words, a language of geometry, frequency, and difference.

Observe the patterns in all things and follow the stories they tell, for much wisdom is hidden in the world, waiting to be discovered.

We are never alone in totality.

What the human eye can see is only but one frequency, of infinite activity and resonance.

The Robin

Every year on the same day
A robin flew near by
The anniversary of her grandmothers death
The questions of reason become unknown
When we look to metaphor and synchronicities
All of which would be considered 'New Age'
But at least it makes you think about
The ones you met on the way
The ones who are no longer here and have gone away
There are some that come into your life
But for whatever reason have become strangers
It can be taken away
But what was meant to stay
Will not lead you astray
Will you make a better person of yourself
I think the right principle is knowing
They were there for a reason
To teach you lessons and experience regressions
This is all a process of unity

Ω

About The Author

Rhys Campbell was born Bermudian, though he grew up in Cardiff, Wales which moulded him to be the person he is today. Self-taught, he started writing for himself at the tender age of 14.

Rhys often conveys his poetry within the verbalised art form that is spoken word. You can find his work on all major streaming platforms usually complemented with ambient instrumentals to further ensure the impact of the narratives illustrated.

@rhysc.ampbell

About The Author

Elijah is a seasoned Light Language artist and Starseed born on the island of Bermuda. With over 9 years of attentive experience in writing Light Language, he has written in hundreds of unique patterns and octaves, at times printing seemingly otherworldly pictographs, with a count-loss at over 3,000 unique portraits of Light Language. His expertise orbits within a solar system of attuned sensitivity toward frequencies of Light Language patterns and multidimensional archetypes within the now local field of my awareness and translating these feelings/sensations into physical formations through writing and art. Currently, he is focused on exploring and writing poetry in his native Earth language and sharing abstract thoughts through the written and spoken word. In his spare time, he enjoys spending time outdoors, reading/literature and tinkering with gardening tech.

Instagram @qbitai

RELEASED BY DARK THIRTY POETRY

ANTHOLOGY ONE
THIS ISN'T WHY WE'RE HERE
MORTAL BEINGS
POEMS THAT WERE WRITTEN ON TRAINS BUT
WEREN'T WRITTEN ABOUT TRAINS
CLOSING SHIFT DREAMS
DESIRE
ANIMATE
THESEUS AND I
I DON'T HAVE THE WORDS FOR THIS
CONVERSATIONS BETWEEN THE SUN AND THE
MOON
SLUT POP
JADED
I'VE BIRTHED AN IDEA OF YOU
BRUISES
CITY GOTHIC
LONG DIVISION
SAY HER NAME
LUMIN

Printed in Great Britain
by Amazon